The Zebra

Striped Horse

text by Christine Denis-Huot
photos by Michel and Christine Denis-Huot

ini Charlesbridge

Library of Congress Cataloging-in-Publication Data
Denis-Huot, Christine
    [le zèbre, cheval rayé. English]
    The zebra: striped horse/text by Christine Denis-Huot;
photographs by Michel and Christine Denis-Huot.
      p.   cm.—(Animal close-ups)
    Includes bibliographical references (p.   )
    Summary: Describes the physical characteristics of the plains
zebra and follows the activities of a zebra herd over the course of
one year as they feed, fight, mate, give birth, search for water, and
encounter other animals on the African plains.
    ISBN 0-88106-882-9 (softcover)
    1. Zebras—Juvenile literature. [1. Zebras.] I. Denis-Huot,
Michel, ill. II. Title. III. Series.
QL737.U62D4513 1999   98-6149
599.665'7—dc21

Plains zebras live in herds in the African savanna. From a distance you can hardly tell the difference between males and females.

During the rains

In the great African plains, the tall grass stretches as far as the eye can see. Only a few umbrella-shaped acacia trees rise above it. It's January, and the zebras share these big open spaces with wildebeests, gazelles, impalas, and other grass-eating animals. These herbivores do well now; there is fresh green grass everywhere.

The zebras gather in herds that can sometimes get very large. They move slowly across the grasslands, grazing.

Zebras may sleep through the midday heat. Some of them only lower their heads, while others lie down. Others keep watch.

Scientists think that zebras are black with white stripes, not white with black stripes.

Zebras can rotate their big ears in every direction to find out where a sound is coming from.

They have big teeth that they use to cut grass.

Their hooves are powerful weapons with hard, sharp edges.

Different stripes

At first, all zebras look alike. But if you look closely, you will see that every stripe pattern is different. The stripes help them recognize the other members of their herd.

Zebras have eyes on the sides of their heads, which let them see in all directions to watch out for danger. They move their big ears to communicate with each other. If they lay them back against their heads, watch out! They're going to bite.

Zebras are only about four or five feet high at the shoulder and can weigh up to seven hundred pounds. A lot of their weight is muscle, making them very fast runners. Like their cousins, the horses, zebras only have one toe on each foot. A protective hoof like a superthick toenail surrounds it.

A tail ending in a black tuft is useful for chasing away annoying insects!

Fierce fighting

In the middle of the herd is a group of young males, called colts, about four or five years old. They have lived together for months, but now it's time for each of them to start his own family. They are becoming stallions, full-grown male zebras.

Wounds can be severe, though the fighters try not to hurt each other too much.

Before they fight, males pull back their lips and smell their opponents. The winner will approach a female and start a family group.

By kneeling down, a stallion protects his legs and belly.

Being strong isn't enough to win a fight—a stallion has to be fast and agile.

One of the colts tries to get close to a female zebra, a mare, but a rival quickly challenges him. They square off for a fight. They bite each other on the throat, neck, and legs until one of them gives up.

The winner approaches the mare, but she isn't interested. He has better luck with another mare. He will have to attract two or three more females before his family is complete.

Thomson's gazelles migrate with zebras because they also need to drink a lot.

Topis share the vast plains with zebras, gazelles, and wildebeests.

During the annual migration, 1 million wildebeasts travel with heards of more than 200,000 zebras.

The great trek

The zebra family moves from one tuft of grass to the next. Because this food is not very nutritious, zebras need to eat a lot. They will even eat dirt to get the minerals they need.

The savanna can feed huge numbers of herbivores because they don't all eat the same food. Zebras eat the top of the long grass while wildebeests and gazelles eat other parts.

Months go by, everything dries out, and food becomes scarce. The zebras have to eat leaves or dig to get at roots and tubers. Water becomes impossible to find. It's time to move to greener pastures.

Together, zebras, wildebeests, and gazelles begin a very long trip.

Danger!

In long, long lines, the zebras move across the plains. Suddenly the stallion screams in alarm—he has seen a pack of wild dogs on the hunt. The family splits up, running in all directions. One mare is surrounded, and her terrified neighs bring the stallion charging back. He keeps the dogs at bay by biting and kicking. Finally he succeeds in bringing the young mare back to the herd.

Not far off, some lionesses ambush and capture an old stallion that strayed out on his own. The weakest prey, usually the young or the old, are easiest to catch. Without seeming afraid, the rest of the zebra herd passes close to the big, feeding cats. They know that for now the lionesses are not a threat.

Some groups of lions specialize in hunting zebras, but others avoid them.

Hyenas hunting in packs can isolate
and catch a zebra.

Only some packs of wild dogs hunt zebras.
They tire them out in long chases.

Crocodiles lie in wait for zebras that
come to the water to drink.

Zebras don't like to swim. They have a hard time keeping their heads and necks out of the water.

Sometimes they stay by the side of a river for days before gathering enough courage to cross.

Rivers are also dangerous for wildebeests. They slip on the steep slopes.

Water!

Zebras' food is so dry that they have to drink every day. This means that they have to stay close to water. What if there isn't any left? Then the animals use their hooves to dig in the bed of a dry river. They may have to dig very deep to reach water.

As they travel, a large river blocks their path, and the zebras gather together on the bank. Restless, they move toward the water but then panic and back up again. They finally cross after several tries, walking in single file, nose to tail.

Once they arrive in green pastures, the animals separate into smaller herds. They will enjoy the new area for several months. Then, one day, it will be time to go back.

Crocodiles catch zebras in the water. Fortunately for zebras, they only eat about 50 meals a year and can even go for two years without eating.

Everyone needs a family

Two stallions pass each other while grazing. To say hello, they sniff at one another's nostrils and stomachs, and then one rubs his head against the other's flank.

Suddenly, the wildebeests nearby start to panic and run in all directions. The zebra family is worried and spreads out too. When they all calm down, one of the mares can't find the rest of the group. She calls for them loudly.

Head raised and lips curled, a zebra smells the air.

Oxpeckers ride on zebras and eat the insects that bother them.

Only members of the same family groom each other with their teeth. They never groom strangers.

Zebras look for dusty ground to clean their coats. They roll on their backs with all four feet in the air.

When the lost mare finds her family, two other mares immediately come over. They gently nibble and scratch her with their teeth, as a sign of friendship. Mares in the same family will stay together even if the stallion leaves or is replaced.

Not far away, one of the mares rolls in the dust. A second and then a third join in—zebras often do the same things at the same time!

Quick, get up!

In February, the rains have made the land green again. One of the pregnant mares lies down to give birth. Her family stays close by to protect her.

As soon as the baby zebra—called a foal—is born, his mother licks him and nibbles at his neck and head. He tries very hard to stand up. Only 15 minutes after he was born, he manages to stay on his feet. Soon he is strong enough to suckle.

Two hours after his birth, the baby can keep up with his mother as she moves around. A few hours later he tries his first short gallop. With all the dangers surrounding him, a foal must quickly learn how to run.

Most babies are born in the rainy season. Food is rich then, and mothers have a lot of milk.

The foal likes to rub his head against his mother.

The newborn weighs about 70 pounds. When he is full-grown, he'll weigh 10 times that amount.

A young foal has to rest more often than adults do. At the smallest cry of alarm, he will jump to his feet.

Foals have light brown stripes that darken as they get older.

Foals get milk from their mothers until they are about seven months old.

Watchful parents

Soon the newborn joins the rest of his family, and the stallion licks and grooms him. The foal gets tired and lies down, while the adults move away. The watchful stallion comes back and bites him gently and then harder and harder until the foal gets up. Then they join the others.

As he gets older, the foal becomes interested in other zebras his age. They race and play-fight together, but they never go far from their mothers. The mares and the stallion are always ready to protect their babies from predators hoping to make a meal of them.

Several months go by, and the foal eats grass now. The mother is expecting another baby. When her young son tries to suckle, she pushes him away. For now, they continue to graze together.

Insects drive a foal to seek shelter under his mother's tail. She will chase away the insects.

A new family

The zebra family has grown bigger. The oldest mare leads the herd when they move from place to place. Walking proudly with his head held high, the stallion looks fierce to keep other males away from his herd.

Many of the foals are now two years old. One of them is a female who is ready to have babies of her own. Her father doesn't chase other stallions away from her now, and he lets one of them start a new herd with her.

Young males leave their birth families to live with other colts. For two years they grow bigger and stronger. When they are about four years old they will start their own families.

Old stallions that can no longer defend their families sometimes join groups of young males.

Zebras in danger

There are several different kinds of zebra, but only the plains zebras are widespread. All the other species are in danger of extinction because of hunting and loss of habitat.

Zebras are the only members of the Equidae family to have stripes. Why? Scientists were puzzled for a long time. They now think that zebras' stripes are linked to the presence of the tsetse fly.

A male zebra and a female horse produce a "zebrule."

Stripes vs. the tsetse fly

Zebras and horses are descendants of the same animal. Their ancient ancestors arrived on the African continent without stripes. They were immediately attacked by tsetse flies, which carry sleeping sickness. A lot of animals died. The survivors evolved. Tsetse flies use their eyes to guide them. Scientists discovered in laboratory tests that alternating bands of black and white confuse them. So stripes may have worked like camouflage to protect the ancient zebras!

Zebras and humans

Zebras can live in captivity as long as their pens are big enough. People have occasionally managed to harness them, but they've never succeeded in taming them like donkeys or horses. Zebras can breed with horses, though this wouldn't normally happen in nature. The offspring of a zebra and a horse can't reproduce. They are sterile, like mules, the offspring of a donkey and a horse.

Still flourishing

Today about 300,000 plains zebras live all over Africa. The big animal reserves in Kenya and Tanzania hold large numbers of them, but they have disappeared from farming and ranching areas. Five very similar subspecies still exist. They are not endangered yet and also are not protected. The quagga zebra is gone forever. This kind of zebra used to live all over southern Africa. But they were killed by farmers and disappeared at the end of the 19th century.

This plains zebra has many more stripes than the quagga had. This may be because it has to deal with many more tsetse flies.

Striped cousins in danger

Other zebra species are endangered. A few Cape Mountain zebras survive in southern Africa. They have been brought back from the brink of extinction. In 1913, only 27 of them remained alive. About 7,000 Hartmann's zebras live under the protection of farmers in the Namibian mountains. The Grévy's zebra lives in the deserts of Ethiopia, Somalia, Sudan, and northern Kenya. Only about 10,000 survive.

To study the Grévy's zebras in the Kenyan Samburu reserve, scientists put radio collars on them.

Close Cousins

Plains zebras are herbivores whose feet are protected from the uneven ground by a case made of horn, called a hoof. They are part of the Equidae family, like the mountain and Grévy's zebras, the donkey, and the horse. All of these animals have only one toe on each foot. Differences among them are small. A zebra has many stripes, but horses and donkeys do not. Donkeys have longer ears and larger heads than horses do.

▲

A few *Somalian donkeys* still exist. They have a black stripe along their backs and stripes on their stomachs, muzzles, and the bottoms of their legs. Wild Asian donkeys don't have any stripes. The Nubian donkey has virtually disappeared. Tame European donkeys are related to wild African donkeys.

◀ *Grévy's zebras* live in the North African deserts. They are very well adapted and are especially tolerant of heat and thirst. They are the biggest zebra. You can recognize them by their big, rounded ears. Their black stripes are narrow and close together and run right down to their hooves. Unlike other zebras, they bray like donkeys. They don't live in families.

The *Przewalski's horse* is a primitive animal, related to one of the ancestors of the domestic horse. It survived in the wild until 1960. Now it lives only in captivity. Scientists are trying to reintroduce these horses in Mongolia. They have excellent endurance. You can recognize them by their blond coats, white noses, and the black stripe down their backs.

◀ The *mountain zebra* is the smallest equine in the world. It lives in southern Africa. Because these zebras are very good climbers, they are well suited to living in the rocky terrain of the mountains. Their hearts are bigger than those of the plains zebra and their hooves are especially hard. You can recognize them by the small pouch of skin that hangs from their necks. They live in families, like the plains zebra.

For Further Reading on Zebras . . .

Arnold, Caroline, <u>Zebra</u>. Photographs by Richard Hewett. New York: William Morrow & Co., 1987.

Lepthien, Emilie U., <u>Zebras</u>. Chicago: Children's Press, 1994.

Markert, Jenny, <u>Zebras</u>. Mankato, MN: Child's World, 1992.

Scuro, Vincent, <u>Wonders of Zebras</u>. New York: Dodd, Mead, 1983.

Interested in Zebras and Other African Animals? Then Read . . .

Lindblad, Lisa, <u>Serengeti Migration: Africa's Animals on the Move</u>. Photographs by Sven-Olaf Lindblad. New York: Hyperion Books for Children, 1994.

To See Zebras in Captivity . . .

Folzenlogen, Darcy and Robert, <u>The Guide to American Zoos and Aquariums</u>. Willow Press, 1993.

To Watch and Learn about Zebra Life on Video, See . . .

<u>Patterns in the Grass</u>. National Geographic Society Special Series. 60 min. Columbia TriStar Home Video, 1993. Not rated.

Use the Internet to Find Out More about Zebras and Other Animals . . .

Herds of Information about Zebras: This is the place to start.
http://www.alumni.caltech.edu/~kantner/zebras

Yahooligans Science Pages
http://www.yahooligans.com/science_and_oddities/animals